ALL MY DAYS

A Personal Life Review

RICHARD P. JOHNSON, PH.D.

Liguori
Lifespan

ONE LIGUORI DRIVE, LIGUORI, MO 63057-9999

Imprimi Potest:
Richard Thibodeau, C.Ss.R.
Provincial, Denver Province
The Redemptorists

ISBN 0-7648-0643-2
Library of Congress Catalog Card Number: 00-100078

Liguori Lifespan is an imprint of Liguori Publications.

To order, call 1-800-325-9521
http://www.liguori.org

Editor: Hans Christoffersen
Cover design by Wendy Barnes

Contents

Foreword

Every life story needs to be told;
every life deserves an autobiography,
including your own!

Your personal life story is an adventure that needs to be lifted up as a unique rendition of how God's love acts in the world.

Your story has all the components of a "spiritual bestseller": brokenness, redemption, forgiveness, transformation, enlightenment, more brokenness, tragedy, confusion, more forgiveness…on and on your life unveils the redemptive work of God.

It's in the second half of life that we truly begin to appreciate the panoramic vistas of our lives and capture their wondrous memories. This is the time when we have the opportunity to start quilting them together into a unique tapestry. It is an opportunity for a labor of love that we couldn't have attempted earlier in life.

Our memories are the "stuff" of our lives—raw material which needs to be organized and arranged so it can be woven into a seamless garment. Writing a personal life review can become our wisdom apparel, our own coat of many colors which proudly proclaims how God's finger has long been on us, guiding each of our lives.

I offer this book as a blueprint for your personal spiritual autobiography. Use it, embrace it, wrestle with it, and you will be creating an autobiography…for yourself, your children, and your children's children. When you complete this book, you will have created a summary of the masterpiece that God created…You!

RICHARD P. JOHNSON, PH.D.
JANUARY 4, 2000

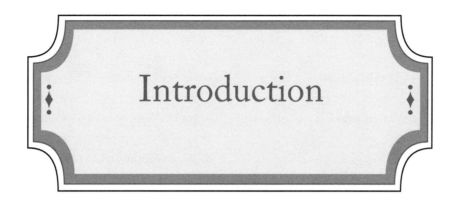

Introduction

Welcome to an experience of a lifetime....

In fact, your lifetime *is* the experience. Traveling the road of life, most of us are kept so busy navigating the road itself that we seldom, if ever, make the time and effort to stop, take stock, and look back. Looking back is not regressive or idle reverie. Looking back on our life in an organized manner can pay dividends in personal understanding that we never before thought possible.

We have headlights on our cars to let us see what's in front of us. In a similar fashion, this book provides "rear lights" which give us the hindsight of seeing where we have been and how we got to where we are today. But hindsight is not always twenty-twenty; sometimes, we need to map things out. This book is intended to help do just that.

A Sharper Image of Ourselves

Our lives seem to be punctuated by times when we seek a deeper understanding of the meaning of our lives. We yearn for clearer perspectives, keener insight, and cleaner values. At such times, we require a sharper image of ourselves and of what is important to us. As we move through our maturing years, we especially wonder what we have learned in our journey of life thus far. We desire a more coordinated view of life, one which reflects the experience we have amassed. We seek ways of converting this experience into something more organized, coordinated, and orderly than its current, somewhat disheveled state.

Our maturing years are sometimes called "the wisdom years." These are the years in which we can unearth treasures of heart and mind, spirit and soul, that have otherwise rested peacefully while awaiting discovery. Our personal life history is the repository of these treasures. Such treasures—when deeply understood and seen through the eyes of faith—provide the underlying outline for our life script. "Wisdom-making" requires that we flesh out and color this underlying script. As we do, we give our lives meaning far beyond what we could have otherwise deciphered: we *find* wisdom!

Some questions immediately arise here: From where do we get the power to transform our lives from a sense of day-to-day survival into an adventure of magnificent proportion? What process is needed to discover the integrating factors which have given our lives a wholeness and completeness that we may not even have realized was there? Through what secret alchemy can we convert our desires for the sweetness of deeper understanding into actual, practical, and enduring principles of wisdom?

Perhaps the most profoundly Christian understanding we could ever develop, as we live out the path of life, is the ever richer recognition that God's finger has been "on us" in every step and turn. God was always there, nudging, whispering in our ear the directions for our next step. As we look back, the profound plan and purpose that we are living out begins to come into clearer focus. A revitalized vision helps us. Even those points

of life we formerly defined as mistakes or tragedies may, in retrospect, show themselves to have been something quite different than our impulsive, first impression thought them to be.

An Autobiography of Faith

How do we initiate this process of positive reminiscing, and direct it in ways which bring us a personal deepening of faith? One of the best ways is through writing. An autobiography of faith starts with our earliest recollections of God-consciousness and proceeds through the decades up to the present moment. In each decade, we can trace the work of the Holy Spirit in our life as the challenges, successes, failures, and even the monotony of our existence unfolded to reveal the lessons we encountered in the "classroom" of life. Writing a chronology of our faith journey will give us a stimulating glimpse of the grand design of our lives that will inspire us as we continue the walk of life.

The goal of all this is to recognize the lessons of love we have learned. God's hand is what gives shape to the lessons of our life. There can be no motivation for these lessons other than God's love. Even the losses we experience, as we march through each succeeding stage of our life, can ultimately be lessons of love. Life is an ongoing adjustment to the succession of losses and gains, and a parade of exchanges between both.

God's love is *the* cohesive and energizing force which ties our lives together and gives us the energy to proceed. God's love is the foundation upon which we build the structure of our lives. As we move through the transitions of life, we are called to revisit this vital fact of God's abiding care by recognizing the divine power working on our behalf along the way.

A Spiritual Autobiography

The ideas our culture instills in us about maturation can be regressive and oppressive if we let them. They lead us to believe that life as a maturing adult is all about protecting and nurturing the body and being myopically concerned with merely the physical dimension of our lives, i.e., what we can see, taste, hear, touch, and smell. As Christians, we know that our lives are so

much more than this. When we add a sense of spirituality to life review, we come up with a completely new concept: spiritual autobiography. A spiritual autobiography is a unique way of discovering and touching our soul with tenderness. Such "soul work" is essential for maturing people of faith because it completes all that a life review otherwise does: It nourishes our inner being, feeds our soul, and renews our spirit; it enhances our ability to perceive beyond the physical structures of our lives, and enriches our relationship with others, ourselves, and God.

Francis Dorff, O.Praem., has written a sensitive book about how to write our spiritual autobiography, *Simply Soulstirring: Writing as a Meditative Process*, (New York, Paulist Press, 1998). This small book (84 pages) succeeds in giving us the theory as well as the practice of spiritual autobiography. Dorff artfully and empathetically convinces us that writing is good for the soul. He maintains that our culture is toxic to our soul development; we must buttress ourselves with meditative practices that can "ground" us spiritually. Meditative writing is one of these practices. He encourages us to write daily. This spiritual discipline can reward us with becoming ever more aware of the hand of God in every moment of our lives. We strengthen our mood, heighten our cheerfulness, and break through hang-ups that may previously have blocked us from seeing the richness and meaning in our daily lives.

Dorff tells us that this kind of meditative life review writing comes from the inner places of our soul, which is what makes this way of writing "simply soul-stirring." When we write in this fashion, we let our *self* get out of the way so that the true "me" can emerge, unfettered by any conspicuous feeling that we have to censor our writing for fear that someone will criticize it. When we write a spiritual autobiography, we write for ourselves. We are on a treasure hunt, searching for evidence in our lives that God has been there, and is still there. These treasures are inside of us, they are waiting to be unearthed, to come to the light of day at a time and a place when (and where) they can be more fully understood than in the past. No longer do they need to be interpreted through our younger, less experienced eyes;

now they can be seen in the fullness of the illuminating light of Jesus.

What are we to write about in our spiritual autobiography? We write about all the dimensions of our lives, both "the personal and the more-than-personal levels of our experience" (Dorff, page 17). We write about the good times, and the times we felt out of balance; the times of forward development, and the times when we thought we slid backwards; we write about the peak experiences, as well as the times when we slogged through the swamps of life. This kind of writing holds the promise of an almost magical emergence of new revelations, of new insights that bubble to the top of our awareness as we delve more deeply into formerly hidden connections between events, the associations among our many relationships that evaded our full perception "back then," and the fabulous interplay among and between all the arenas of our life.

Most of all, we write about our movement from one phase and stage of life to another. We identify the forces and powers that nudged us one way or another, leading us down some roads and pulling us away from others. All of this, and so much more, becomes the subject of our personal inquiry into ourselves. Ultimately, we begin to discern what Dorff calls the "integrating rhythm" (page 17) of our lives, i.e., the beat of our own developmental drum, which strikes a beat so steady and sure that it creates the cadence for our journey of personal development and spiritual growth. When we sense this deeply unifying and undergirding theme running through our lives, i.e., when we come to a keener understanding of it all, we quite naturally ask: "Who is the one beating the drum?"

Writing a spiritual autobiography helps us awaken to the wonder-full *process* of our lives, rather than seeing only the results of our actions. So often, our culture solely focuses on what we produce, achieve, and accomplish. Such a perspective is denigrating to any adult person. It especially trivializes and discounts the maturing years on the basis of the "productive" years being in the past. Such a perspective contorts the real purpose of life, which is the flowering of the whole person in the ongoing process of life. A product-centered world-view makes us blind to the magnificent wholeness of day-to-day life, the fortifying "being" of life.

Writing a spiritual autobiography will help us to discern more clearly the underlying unity in our lives. Eventually, we come to the profound awareness that there is now—and always has been—a golden thread running through everything in our lives. This understanding generates within us a silent solace of security in our senior years. This security lets us know that we are gently cradled in God's hands all along our journey of life.

Developmental Tasks

In each phase of life, we encounter tasks which we must accomplish before we can confidently and completely move on to the next phase. In order to grow from one stage to another, we must master the appropriate developmental tasks of that particular stage. In order to move from childhood into adolescence, for example, we must accomplish many developmental tasks. We must learn to walk, care for our bodily needs, communicate, and reason in an elementary way, etc. Likewise, movement from adolescence into young adulthood means that we must learn to support ourselves, develop close relationships with others, shoulder responsibility, develop a fundamental philosophy of life, and an abiding faith in God. In order to move successfully through middle adulthood, we must confront our mortality, form deeper relationships with others, learn how to shift relationships with friends, relatives, and loved ones, widen our faith in God, and sharpen our focus on things spiritual.

The "stages of life" listed on the next page outline the phases of life, arranged in decades and named in a convenient fashion. Our personal journey of life can be seen as the story of how we encountered, addressed, and mastered the many developmental tasks through each life stage. The questions in this book are crafted from the developmental tasks of a lifetime. Taken together, they constitute a vast overview of the "life work" each one of us needs to perform so that we can move forward by the developmental imperative and God's illuminating light.

The Stages of Life

1. THE FORMATIVE YEARS: .... CHILDHOOD .... BIRTH TO 10

2. TEENAGE TURMOIL: .... ADOLESCENCE .... 11 TO 20

3. BECOMING AN ADULT: .... YOUNG ADULTHOOD .... 21 TO 30

4. COMING INTO YOUR OWN: .... EARLY ADULTHOOD .... 31 TO 40

5. HITTING THE WALL: .... MIDDLE ADULTHOOD .... 41 TO 50

6. LAYING A NEW FOUNDATION: .... LATE-MIDDLE ADULTHOOD .... 51 TO 60

7. FINDING NEW DRIVE: .... EARLY MATURE ADULTHOOD .... 61 TO 70

8. DEVELOPING A NEW VISION: ..... MATURE ADULTHOOD .... 71 TO 80

9. THE WONDER YEARS: .... SENIOR MATURE ADULTHOOD .... 81 PLUS

Benefits of Reminiscence

As we proceed in our personal life review, and as we transform our thoughts and reminiscences into a faith autobiography, we invite into our lives those virtues that build an enriched character and expand our spiritual depth. The benefits of our work of reminiscence are the very fruits we are promised, the fruits of the Holy Spirit.

A peaceful wisdom rises from a review of the life of faith. This wisdom has many dimensions. It is a wisdom that allows us to use the accumulated knowledge of a lifetime in loving service of a clearer insight into the true reality of our earthly experience. Such a wisdom illuminates our inner qualities and recognizes the presence of God in ourselves and in all things. In so doing, wisdom gifts us with a spiritual intuition that enables us to see love everywhere, especially the handiwork of God's love acting in our life. A prayerful life review process guides us along a prudent course toward the goal of loving God more completely.

What is the purpose of all this memory work we call life review? What can come of it that is positive for the soul? In a word, plenty! In the book *Guiding Autobiography Groups for Older Adults: Exploring the Fabric of Life* (Johns Hopkins University Press, Baltimore, 1991), Donna E. Deutchman and James E. Birren illuminate a number of positive outcomes. Life review allows us to:

- throw away any of our attitudinal "antiques"
- perceive our present life more accurately
- take on increased personal responsibility
- develop a more defined personal "future"
- decrease our encumbering denial
- itemize our successful coping strategies
- polish our self-image
- move toward reconciliation more smoothly
- develop new and clearer meaning for our life experiences

- increase our self-understanding and personal acceptance
- construct a more comprehensive self-definition
- express our authentic self better

This list establishes the goals of any therapeutic relationship, and each one of these items is what is hoped for in therapy. The personal consequences of such marvelous life tasks are enormous. The idea that these goals can be accomplished from working one's life review into an autobiography is nothing short of a developmental "coup."

A Rich Process

The best—and easiest—method we have of gleaning the miracle of life is to ask our memories finely crafted questions, i.e., questions which plumb our depths and define our spiritual core. These are questions that can be used to help ground us in—and clarify for us—each stage of life.

Such incisive questions are the core of this book, the stimuli that will motivate us to dig deeply into our life and harvest the wonder that lays there for the taking. Earnestly working to answer these questions brings us ever closer to our goal of spiritual integration. Spiritual integration means being able to look back over our entire life span and say: "This has been good! To be sure, I have made mistakes along the way, but I now see that even these mistakes allowed me to grow in ways I would otherwise not have been able to." Such an attitude is the mark of spiritual maturity.

Lessons of Love Learned: The Questions of Life

This book is a compendium of questions which have been carefully crafted. They have been formulated from the developmental tasks of the decades and lessons of the life course. Each of eight decades has been divided into six life arenas:

1. School/career/work
2. Family
3. Relationship
4. Self
5. Leisure
6. Spirit

Within each arena, you will find five questions. This means there are thirty questions exploring each decade. The book as a whole, therefore, has a total of two hundred and forty questions.

The sequence of the questions is designed in a special way. Proceeding with the questions in the order given will automatically lead you to create an autobiography of your life. You can think of each decade as a new chapter in your life, and the life arenas as subheadings.

What Are the Six Life Arenas?

Try to conceive of your life laid out as a three-ring circus; instead of having three rings, however, the "circus" of your life has six. At one and the same time, you are performing different roles in each of the six rings. We call each ring a life arena—an area of your life, where you perform—balance—certain tasks and roles.

1. *The life arena of school/career/work*

    Anything you do which is job-related is in this life arena. All vocational training or education is in your career arena. Your career or job is always changing even if you stay in the same job, because the way you perform your job—as well as your thoughts about yourself in that job—is constantly changing. Many who do not work outside of the home still perform many job functions that give them an active career arena. For example, a homemaker does not work outside of the home, yet he or she performs many jobs and chores. The management of the house and all the tasks performed to maintain the house and help all the persons living in the house are career life tasks.

    In addition, some who have retired may have a difficult time thinking that they still have a work or career arena, but they certainly do! They may volunteer their time and talents, pursue a burning passion that consumes them, perform grandchild care tasks, work in their church, or any other number of social, civic, fraternal, and political organizations. All of this work can be considered an extension of the career arena.

2. *The life arena of family*

Most people were born into a family and learned a vast amount of information in that family. All that you learned, good and otherwise, is contained in your family arena. All your interactions between and among your brothers and sisters, mother and father, aunts, uncles, cousins, etc., are family arena material. Your various roles in the family arena have also changed over the years. In your early years, you needed your parents for assistance. As you grew and matured, this dependent role gradually evolved toward greater independence: You gradually took on more and more responsibility for yourself. This is the family life arena, a story this book will help you bring to light.

3. *The life arena of relationship*

Relationships have to do with sharing. This third life arena contains all the sharing you perform with people outside your family. You share yourself with many people, some in very casual and fleeting ways, others much more intimately. You have a range of friends and acquaintances, and it is the quality and depth of your sharing with these people that constitutes the "stuff" of the relationship life arena. You have some level of relationship with the bank teller, the waitress, the gas station attendant, your caregivers. As you move along the spectrum of relationships, however, you begin to share more and more of yourself, from acquaintances to colleagues, friends, good friends, close friends, best friends, confidants, and finally to the one person with whom you have the most intimate relationship. There's a lot of living that goes on in the relationship arena, and this book helps you to remember and clarify all that living.

4. *The life arena of self*

Whereas the relationship arena is concerned with sharing yourself exteriorly, the life arena of self focuses on how you relate with yourself: your self-concept and your relationship with your body. All that happens inside of your internal self, your thoughts, feelings, and emotions, is in this life arena. Actually, you have many self-concepts about what you are and how you do things. You also have many relationships with your body, what you can do with your body, and how it functions.

5. *The life arena of leisure*

All that you like to do when you don't have to do anything else is contained in the leisure arena. Fun and play, hobbies and sports, relaxation and rest, enlightenment for your mind, and just plain doing nothing are components of the leisure life arena. Tennis and checkers, fishing and walking, playing cards and watching ball games are leisure arena activities.

Play is to the leisure arena what work is to the career arena. You need both—they are opposite sides of the same coin. You do things in the leisure arena because you want to, not because you ought to, are expected to, or directed to: You do it for the sheer pleasure of it. You are the sole director of your leisure arena. Play is a big part of life, and this book helps you to grasp the full meaning and fun of just playing.

6. *The life arena of spirit*

Each of us has a relationship with God. Even a person who doesn't believe in God has some concept of order or ultimate reason. Your conception of—and relationship with—God or a higher order is what makes up the spirit life arena. Your sense of awe and wonder, surprise and excitement, your creative self and your understanding self, are all parts of the spirit arena. Your dimensions of quiet and prayerfulness, religiosity, and care are roles you perform in this arena.

There is a natural overlap among and between these six life arenas, but the questions that follow are formulated to enrich your present life by tapping into your past experiences in ways that are enjoyable, meaningful, and clarifying.

Writing Hints

1. There is absolutely no rush in writing your autobiography, take as long as you wish. You can write your autobiography in the comfort and solitude of your own home or take it with you into a retreat setting. You may even wish to join with a couple of close friends who wish to write their own autobiographies along with you: Gathering each week to share your writing to date can be a tremendously enriching and intimate experience for all concerned.

2. Try to get into your feelings. As much as possible, try to respond to the questions not simply with the bare facts, but with your honest feelings. Your feelings are the movers of the drama of your life. In addition to "thought memory," we all have a "feelings memory" of all the emotions associated with a particular event or relationship. Unearthing these feelings will give depth and drama to your writing and add dimensions of development that will enrich you along the way. Feelings make writing down your responses an adventure rather than a chore.

3. Expand on the questions. The questions are only general guidelines of inquiry. Feel free to change the wording of the questions to better suit your particular setting and circumstances. You are the author of this work, so please go beyond the questions. See the questions merely as invitations to explore all the facets of your life.

4. It is OK to go back over questions and responses you have already covered. As you make your way through the questions, you may recall more details or feelings about situations about which you have already written. Go back and add to those points,

make the images that are now coming back to you more clearly complete the picture.

5. Feel free to change the "tense" of the questions. All the questions in each of the decades are written in the past tense, except for the chapter on "ages seventy and beyond" which is written in the present tense. Use the tense that is right for your life stage. For example, if you are sixty-three years old, then change the tense of the questions in your current decade to the present tense.

6. Project into the future. If you like, you can respond to questions in decades that you haven't yet reached by projecting how you imagine you would like to respond to that question when you do reach that age.

7. Change questions to suit your situation. You may find some questions that do not pertain to you, for example, questions about married life or children are obviously not pertinent if you have not been married or had any children. Please feel free to change the questions to "fit" you. The point is to engage the *spirit* of the question, not its specific content. For example, you may need to change the word "spouse" to "friend," or "marriage" to "relationship."

8. Of special interest is the school/career/work arena. Persons who have not worked outside the home may think that they have had no career, per se. This couldn't be more inaccurate. Running a household is definitely a career in itself, and must be seen as such when responding to these questions.

Create a Family Heirloom

Completing this personal life review creates a family heirloom. Don't you wish that you had autobiographies of some of your forebears, especially your parents? What a treasure these would be! But you are not simply writing your autobiography for others; indeed, the major benefit of your autobiography is for yourself.

As illustrated above, the process of life review generates so many benefits for you on a variety of emotional, psychological, and spiritual levels. There is no end to the gifts that writing your own autobiography will bestow upon you.

Integration of self is the primary task of our maturing years. Reminiscence is an active process. It is not a turning away from present realities, but rather a "tuning in" to the context of the *now* of our lives so that we may comprehend more fully the vibrant progression of growth that our life has been thus far. Reminiscence allows us to engage more fully in the drama of our lives and retrieve maximum meaning, purpose, and understanding.

Enjoy!

Chapter One
The Formative Years
BIRTH TO AGE TEN

The first decade of my life started on the day of my birth, which was _____.

Memories of our childhood years are of particular importance. Many of them are snippets of fuller life stories, holding for us the promise of deeper understanding. We do well to pay close attention to our memories, investigate them, turn them around in our minds, flesh them out, and thus make them more real. Dismissing any memory would be a mistake, since it would be a missed opportunity for understanding one's life. It would push away unfinished business that now yearns for reconsideration. We try to discern the central theme of the story and determine what significance the theme of the story had for our life at the time when it was first "lived out." Finally, we seek understanding as to what it could mean in our lives now as we review it. By doing this, we connect the memory with our life story.

It has long been recognized that, in times of transition, memories of long ago bounce into our minds without conscious effort or forewarning. As these memories come into our minds, we wonder where they came from, how they got there, and why they are appearing now! They seem random, without context, haphazard, and quite without any sense at all. Researchers have studied this phenomenon, and now speak in common voice when they assert that such memories are not random at all. They are, instead, quite purposeful from a psychological perspective.

So often we are trying to fit together pieces of our lives that formerly seemed disjointed. We may not even be consciously aware of this. In our childhood years, we didn't seek the meaningful connections that may have served to undergird our lives. It may only be in our maturing years, with its budding wisdom, that some internal urge motivates us to recognize and clarify the formerly unknown unifying quality of our childhood. Not until our maturing years, with its enhanced vision and hindsight, are we able to appreciate the themes of each stage of our lives and put these themes into some overarching sequence and order which gives meaning to our lives now.

There are some childhood memories that burst onto our internal "screen" which seem to have little if any connection to anything else at all. It may not even be the mental image of the memory that catches us off guard—it's more the feeling associated with it. The feeling returns until we are all but forced to deal with it. We can do this by feeding the emotion of the memory more fully by placing it in its original context. Recurrent feelings from the past may be attempts by the unconscious part of our mind to find resolution for a feeling that may have been very important at the time, but which, for one reason or another, was figuratively pushed aside, laying unresolved for years until it broke through the surface tension of our mind, thereby finding expression.

15

School/Career/Work Life Arena

> The first decade of life is where we learn a surprising number of work-related values and beliefs. We learn about ourselves as future "workers." Many of these values come as a consequence of our work in school. This mindset about ourselves—and the reactions we received from our elementary work efforts, habits, and accomplishments—is pressed into the soft clay of our minds and form a core foundation that has surprising resiliency across the life span.

1. *What is your earliest recollection of working alongside your father or mother? Describe the situation as detailed as you can.*

   _____

   _____

   _____

   _____

   _____

   _____

2. *Were you responsible for any chores (household, farming, etc.) when you were this young? Describe.*

   _____

   _____

   _____

   _____

3. *What kind of "messages" or "under-the-table" instructions did you receive from your family about your future occupation or manner of how to handle work?*

   _____

   _____

   _____

   _____

   _____

4. *What was your father's primary occupation during this decade of your life? your mother's? What did you think about these jobs then? now? What work-related attitudes do you think you learned from them?*

   _____

   _____

   _____

   _____

   _____

5. *What did you think of school during this time of your life? Describe several school incidents that stick in your mind.*

   _____

   _____

   _____

"The first decade of life is where we learn a surprising number of work-related values and beliefs."

Family Life Arena

Our family life arena is the most important in our first decade of life. So much happens in our family. It's here we learn about social roles, about loving behavior, about caring, compassion, social norms, acceptable (and unacceptable) behavior, expectations, how to get what we want, and so much more. We develop impressions about ourselves through the way we were treated in our family of origin, our place in the birth order of siblings, and more. We learn by either *modeling* the behavior of others, or by *reacting* to behavior that is distasteful to us.

1. How did your family get along? What were the relationships like between each child and your parents? Describe using as much detail as possible.

_____

_____

_____

_____

_____

2. Recall several pleasant memories of your interactions with your family.

_____

_____

_____

_____

_____

3. Were there any crises, transitions, or tragedies that your family faced during this time in your life? If so, describe the experience(s).

_____

_____

_____

_____

_____

4. What do you recall of your family's financial situation at this time? Describe the lasting impact it may have had on you.

_____

_____

_____

_____

5. How prominent in your life were your aunts, uncles, and grandparents during this decade? Give examples.

_____

_____

_____

_____

"We learn by either modeling the behavior of others, or by reacting to behavior that is distasteful to us."

Relationship Life Arena

Friends became increasingly important during this decade. From first grade (or kindergarten or even pre-school) onward, you came in contact with an increasing circle of peers, some of whom you were closer to than others. You gradually built up more and more sharing with others, until you had your first taste of intimate sharing of your internal self. This decade became a story of you creating ever widening circles of interaction with people farther from your home base. These developing relationships taught you a lot and formed much of the basis for your patterns of interaction for years to come.

1. *Who were your friends during these years, and what did you learn from each of them? Describe these people and events.*

_____

_____

_____

_____

_____

2. *With whom did you have the closest, non-family adult relationship during your childhood? Describe this relationship.*

_____

_____

_____

_____

_____

3. *Did you have any close relationships with pets during your childhood?*

_____

_____

_____

_____

_____

_____

4. *What is the most humorous incident you can recall happening with your childhood friends? the most tragic?*

_____

_____

_____

_____

_____

_____

5. *To what degree did your parents share themselves emotionally? Could they demonstrate their feelings? Describe.*

_____

_____

_____

_____

_____

"This decade became a story of you creating ever widening circles of interaction with people farther from your home base."

Self Life Arena

The self life arena in the first years of life have to do with how you felt about yourself as an emerging person, and how you felt about your growing body. Certainly, the "story" of the first decade of life is the unfolding story of your progressive relationship with yourself. Your "self-talk" began in an elementary manner, but the impressions of yourself that you carved out in this first decade were to impact upon your development as an adult. So many of your self-impressions were tied up with your emerging body concept. Your friends were described as "big" or "little," and it appeared to you that the sum total of who you were during this decade was dependent upon your body.

1. *Did you think of yourself as a good daughter or a good son during this time in your life? Why? Try to cite specific examples.*

_____

_____

_____

_____

_____

2. *Were you pleased with your performance in school during these years? Cite specific examples.*

_____

_____

_____

_____

3. *How dependent or independent were you as a child? Try to give specific examples.*

_____

_____

_____

_____

_____

_____

_____

4. *Did you consider yourself a happy person during this decade? What is your assessment now on this?*

_____

_____

_____

_____

_____

5. *What was your most prized possession during this period? Describe the meaning it had for you.*

_____

_____

_____

_____

"Certainly, the 'story' of the first decade of life is the unfolding story of your progressive relationship with yourself."

Leisure Life Arena

Leisure meant play in this decade. Play was an exceedingly important focus of your life, because it was the way you investigated the world, explored your environment, made friends, found success, and how you learned to deal with failure. You learned self-discipline and team effort in play, you learned supervision and direction in play, you learned achievement and accomplishment in play. It was through play that you developed much of the self-definition so important down through the following decades.

1. Describe in detail your favorite childhood play activities and play places.

_____

_____

_____

_____

_____

2. What did you do during your summers off from grade school? Describe, using specific examples.

_____

_____

_____

_____

_____

3. What sports did you play? Which was your favorite? Which provided you the most success? Describe.

_____

_____

_____

_____

_____

_____

4. Did you participate in Cub Scouts, Brownies, 4-H, or any other similar type groups? Describe your experiences.

_____

_____

_____

_____

_____

5. How did your family celebrate holidays in your house, e.g., Thanksgiving, Christmas, Easter, Fourth of July, etc.? Describe.

_____

_____

_____

_____

_____

Spirit Life Arena

Personal spirituality is your ongoing relationship with God. In childhood, you were probably exposed to some level of religious training, usually through church, school, and/or home. The extent of this varied from family to family, yet at some point during this decade you most likely experienced your first "encounter" with God. These questions request that you delve deeply into this period and retrieve whatever had a bearing on your spiritual and religious development. To what degree has this early exposure to church, God, and religious training had a continuing effect upon your life?

1. Describe early memories you have of how your family worshiped.

_____

_____

_____

_____

_____

2. Did you feel that you had a close relationship with God during this phase in your life? Describe. For what did you pray?

_____

_____

_____

_____

_____

3. How would you describe your early spiritual or religious training?

_____

_____

_____

_____

_____

_____

4. Looking back at your childhood, what was God's greatest blessing to you? Describe as thoroughly as possible.

_____

_____

_____

_____

_____

5. Recall and describe an experience from your childhood where you felt particularly close to God.

_____

_____

_____

_____

_____

_____

"Personal spirituality is your ongoing relationship with God."

Chapter Two
Teenage Turmoil
AGES TEN TO TWENTY

My tenth birthday was on _____ .

Most significant historical events that occurred during this decade:

_____

_____

_____

_____

_____

With vision gained from reminiscing about our earliest years, we can now take the next developmental step toward personal integration, and perhaps begin to recognize that behind the seemingly random twists and turns of life, the invisible hand of God is at work. The celestial artist of all life has been there with us all along, designing the plan and guiding our progress as our human hand stitched and tucked the fabric, chose and blended the colors, and wove and hemmed the garment to fit us.

Certainly, there were times in our teen years (and beyond) when we made mistakes; perhaps we even failed in sinful ways. Positive reminiscing, however, affords us a new vision of the past that allows us to recognize that even these "mistakes"—perhaps these mistakes in particular—taught us more of what it means to be the individual person that we are. In ever more profound ways, we come to appreciate the variety and the unique gifts that God bestows upon us.

How often have you been surprised when thoughts of your teenage years appear out of thin air? Suddenly, and seemingly out of nowhere, a memory of a past event from your teen years, a feeling, situation, relationship, or place will jump into your consciousness. It's as if a long-closed file drawer inexplicably slides open to reveal its forgotten treasure. There seems no logic or purpose behind this uninvited guest from the past, yet its arrival is impossible to ignore.

We are left to wonder about the mission of this visitor. Sometimes, the memory seems like an intruder, bent on disturbing our countenance with disrupting feelings of fear, shame, guilt, or sadness. At other times, the remembrance feels like an angelic messenger of peace, joy, love, and serenity. From where do these internal

snapshots of times gone by emerge? What meaning, if any, do they convey?

Those who study such phenomena have recognized that reminiscing is a natural and very healthy behavior which can pay many dividends. Psychologists call the process "life review," and they tell us that the process appears to intensify—thoughts of the past occur with greater frequency—during times of personal change, lifestyle shift, or other kinds of transition.

The kind of reminiscence we are talking about is not the idle wanderings of a disorganized mind, nor is it a means to withdraw from a disagreeable present, nor even an attempt to avoid something unpleasant by retreating into wishful thinking or fantasy. On the contrary, reminiscence is a way to look back over one's life, re-viewing what has come before, and integrating it into a complete picture, thereby giving one's life more meaning, purpose, and direction.

Reminiscence is an effective way to gain a more objective perspective on oneself, and to piece together an understanding on one's life path as a more ordered and unified journey, rather than a disjointed conglomeration of unrelated happenings.

With this insight, we can actively use reminiscence to enhance the richness of the present. We can grow in our appreciation of the people, events, learning, and relationships we have experienced. We see better the unique contribution each has made, and gain insight into the patterns of our own lives. Reminiscence makes us both the artist of this work of art called life and the one viewing its beauty and gleaning its insights.

School/Career/Work Life Arena

School was *the* central focus of our teen years. It took on a more important aspect than it had in the previous decade since it became much more vocationally oriented. We began asking why we were going to school…what was its practical use? This aspect of school became more prominent as we moved through the grades. School appeared more and more as a training ground, or at least a preparation for a lifetime of work. We needed to make vocational decisions, and it seemed that it was school that provided us with the launching pad for this lifetime career.

1. Who was your primary work role model during your teen years? Describe.

2. Recall and describe the part-time jobs that you may have had during this time.

3. Were your parents "grooming" you for any particular career or occupation? Describe why you think so, or think not.

4. Describe experiences during your teen years which may have impacted upon your eventual career/ occupational decision.

5. In what ways did the community in which you were raised have an influence on your eventual occupational choice? Describe.

"School appeared more and more as a training ground, or at least a preparation for a lifetime of work."

Family Life Arena

Your ears were always open during your teen years to the comings and goings, the patterns of interaction, the developing relationships, as well as the rules and expectations that flew around your family constantly. You learned so much from the family during this time. You learned family cohesiveness, i.e., how a family is to support and help one another. You learned adaptability, i.e., how family members encouraged one another to become unique, individual persons. You learned communication skills, i.e., how to relate thoughts and feelings in a context that was respectful, warm, and genuine. All of this—and so much more—became your family life curriculum during your teen years.

1. *To what degree were you free to express personal thoughts and feelings in your family during your teens? Explain.*

_____

_____

_____

_____

_____

2. *Were you closer to your mother or to your father during your teen years? Explain.*

_____

_____

_____

_____

3. *Were there many rules (written or unwritten) in your family at this time? Were these rules open for negotiation?*

_____

_____

_____

_____

_____

4. *How, and by whom, were family decisions made in your family during these years? Describe.*

_____

_____

_____

_____

5. *How difficult was the initial separation from your family when the time came? Describe the experience.*

_____

_____

_____

_____

Relationship Life Arena

Your friends, acquaintances, school mates, etc., gradually became the most important groups for you in your teen years. As you moved through this decade, you looked less to your family—and more to your peers—for approval, recognition, energy, and affirmation. Certainly, the family arena remained strong, but you were becoming increasingly independent as the years passed, and there were probably more than several occasions when your thoughts and desires clashed with the desires of your parents. These clashes created the tension which allowed you to grow with self-discipline and self-confidence.

1. *Were you smooth and self-assured, or awkward and unsure, in social situations during your teen years? Explain.*

_____

_____

_____

_____

_____

2. *Recall and describe your romantic relationships during your teen years.*

_____

_____

_____

_____

_____

3. *Who were the persons with whom you shared the most during your teen years? Explain.*

_____

_____

_____

_____

_____

_____

4. *Try to recall the names of your close friends, and describe your relationship with each of them.*

_____

_____

_____

_____

_____

_____

5. *What types of socializing did you and your friends do? Describe.*

_____

_____

_____

_____

"Your friends, acquaintances, school mates, etc., gradually became the most important groups for you in your teen years."

Self Life Arena

Your teen years brought a real cauldron of bubbling emotions and thoughts about yourself to the fore. These awkward years were all about walking the path from childhood into young adulthood. Throughout the walk, you questioned your qualifications for adulthood almost daily. Peer groups became so important precisely because you were continuously questioning and comparing how you were doing on your developmental path. Contradictory feelings, clashing values, conflicting beliefs, disharmonious feelings, wavering decisions, and faltering actions were more the norm than the exception for most. Somehow you emerged from the teenage turmoil fairly unscathed and ready to tackle the next decade.

1. How were you able to handle criticism during these years? How does this compare to how you handle criticism today?

2. Did you feel like you were a part of the "in-group," or did you feel more or less on your own? Explain.

3. To what degree was it easy for you to get "hurt feelings" during this time? Explain.

4. How did you rate yourself in the areas of appearance, personality, intelligence, success, and status? Try to recall specific examples of each.

5. How easy or difficult was it for you to discuss your weaknesses, inadequacies, or shortcomings? How does this compare to today? Explain.

Leisure Life Arena

Your free time evolved from the awe and wonder of your first decade into exploration of yourself in the second. You explored your power, agility, success in sports, and deepening social relations. You explored your social development in your relationships. You explored your relationship with the larger community in participation with groups and organizations. You explored your sense of freedom and independence in trips and increasing separation from parents. All of this was happening "along the way" as you devoted your free time to a wide spectrum of activities and reveries. It wouldn't be until retirement that you could devote such a percentage of your total available time to leisure activities.

1. *What were your favorite free time activities during your teen years? Describe.*

_____

_____

_____

_____

_____

2. *What was a typical Saturday night like? Try to recall some specific activities and events.*

_____

_____

_____

_____

_____

3. *Did you have a car during your teen years? Describe it and your "relationship" to it.*

_____

_____

_____

_____

_____

_____

4. *Did you take part in any kind of social, civic, fraternal, or religious organizations? Describe.*

_____

_____

_____

_____

_____

_____

5. *What kind of things might you have done in your free time that your parents didn't approve of? Are there any secrets? Explain…if your dare!*

_____

_____

_____

_____

_____

_____

"Your free time evolved from the awe and wonder of your first decade into exploration of yourself in the second."

Spirit Life Arena

Like most teens, you probably covered lots of interior ground weighing, surveying, evaluating, assessing, and sometimes even judging the faith precepts that were part of your childhood. Hopefully, the faith that you emerged with at age twenty was vastly different than the one with which you entered this decade. You were not alone in this. Your friends were going through much the same process, some more publicly than others. You may have discussed your thoughts, questions, and insights with them. You may even have had a spiritual mentor who would act as a sounding board, listening as you bartered with God and with yourself.

1. *Describe the spiritual changes that took place in you during this emotionally stormy decade.*

_____

_____

_____

_____

_____

2. *To what degree, if any, did guilt play a role in your spiritual development? Explain.*

_____

_____

_____

_____

_____

3. *What and who did you pray for during your teen years? Explain.*

_____

_____

_____

_____

_____

4. *Who was your most impressive spiritual guide or model during your teen years? Explain.*

_____

_____

_____

_____

_____

5. *What was your most significant experience of this decade? Describe.*

_____

_____

_____

_____

"Hopefully, the faith that you emerged with at age twenty was vastly different than the one with which you entered this decade."

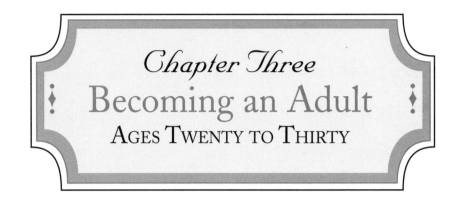

Chapter Three
Becoming an Adult
AGES TWENTY TO THIRTY

The third decade of my life began on my twentieth birthday, which

was on _____.

The major historical events of these ten years were:

_____

_____

_____

_____

_____

We have written on our hearts and minds all of our lives. During our twenties, we recorded mountains of data into our memory bank, containing all we experienced during that momentous decade: what we believed, our thoughts, our feelings, a compilation of all our decisions, and an itemization of all that we did. All this information is in a form that scientific researchers would call "raw material," the data is simply laying there, unorganized, unassessed, and unused. For these reasons, it lacks cohesive meaning, and we won't gain any particular insight or wisdom from it. In order for wisdom to emerge from this mass of information, it must first be "processed": analyzed, inspected, sorted, and arranged in ways that allow us to decipher the true meaning of what's there.

This evaluation process is called "crunching the data." When applied here, we call it life review. Life review is the process where we intentionally sort through the reams of data stored in the memory banks of our mind, and gradually bring each piece of data to light. Similar to working a crossword puzzle, we pick a piece of personal data, inspect it, gain some idea of where it might "fit" into the larger pattern of our lives. Unlike a crossword puzzle, however, where we are given a frame for the individual pieces and the finished product, there are no such indications when trying to sort out the themes or schemata of our life. We can pick up a piece, only to lay it back down again without gaining the slightest notion of where it might belong. Time and again, we handle the same piece, turn it, compare it to other pieces, assess possibilities, all the while trying to gain some understanding of an overall plan of meaning, or blueprint into which the piece might fit.

In our maturing years, we search with more intentionality for the meaning of life. We long to grasp the overarching plan we have been following without too much conscious realization. We yearn to see the map we have been following which gives perspective and sense. We feel the angst of frustration from walking blindly on in our quest for meaning, trying to discover the unifying themes, the coordinating forces, the synthesizing patterns that can somehow be combined into a picture of our life which makes us understand ourselves.

The picture of our life gradually emerges as we discover the rightful places for the puzzle pieces. We come to fuller appreciation of the fact that life is directed by a grand design. Ultimately, an intricate puzzle begins to take shape, and we come to understand that we have been constructing a masterpiece all along. This masterpiece is our life.

For a Christian the grand design is of God. The plan we have been following belongs to God. Certainly, we have deviated from the plan at times, and strayed from the design. Our human egos are tempted to see gaps or holes in the puzzle of life, places where we refused to let God lead us through difficult times. Yet God has taken care of us even there, and it is in these apparent holes that God offers us divine forgiveness. God's forgiveness fills the gaps and holes of our life puzzle with healing grace. In the light of divine forgiveness, we no longer see only gaps and holes, but also the shimmering beauty of God's hand which serves as the cohesive "glue" holding all the surrounding pieces of our "life puzzle" together. God always fills our own human holes and ultimately makes us whole…if we let God in!

School/Career/Work Life Arena

During our twenties, we explore this arena intensely. We generally choose a job, a line of work, even settle into a career. We search for career training and education. We experience trial and error, entry and exit. We begin to settle down, and feel the first sensations of establishing a life of our own. We evaluate and reevaluate our lives. We bring change into our lives like never before, and we move toward various forms of commitment. We envision possibilities, seek mentors and models. Through it all, we generate lots of energy.

1. *Describe how you related to bosses or supervisors during this decade.*

2. *Describe how you made your occupational/career choices during this decade. Add as much detail as possible.*

3. *Describe several work-related incidents from this decade that stick out in your mind.*

4. *Who were the people you modeled yourself after in your career arena during this time? What did you see as attractive in them?*

5. *What were your "career/life dreams" during this time. Describe.*

"We bring change into our lives like never before, and we move toward various forms of commitment."

Family Life Arena

This is the decade where most of us first establish ourselves apart from our family of origin. We begin to carve out a lifestyle environment of our own making. We take on home management, we venture out into financial management for the first time. For many, it's a time of selecting a life mate. We begin our path toward security on many fronts. Many establish a family, and shoulder the weighty role of a parent. We become an adult in the community, with all that goes with that.

1. Describe how you made the transition from your family of origin to becoming an independent person. How difficult or easy was this for you?

2. Describe the first independent household that you established. How did it feel doing so, and how did you feel once you had accomplished it?

3. Describe decisive days/events of this decade, e.g., your wedding day, religious profession, decision to stay single. How did you feel? Explain.

4. What do you remember about the day your first child was born? If you were not a parent during this decade: How did you relate to children when you were in your twenties?

5. Describe several memorable events from your family life during this decade. Try to be specific.

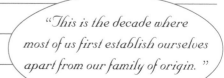

"This is the decade where most of us first establish ourselves apart from our family of origin."

Relationship Life Arena

Our twenties are filled with establishing social networks different and more substantial than those in our teens. Our ability to communicate on a more personal level is generally enhanced during this decade. Broad friendships, while still very important, make room for a major concentration on intimacy development. Much energy is spent on courting, and developing a trusting, caring, sharing, and loving relationship. We learn the relationship skills of negotiating, developing, and communicating expectations, as well as to compromise, support, show compassion and respect.

1. *What type of socializing did you like to do in your twenties? With whom did you socialize? Describe.*

_____

_____

_____

_____

_____

_____

2. *Did you ever "go steady" with someone other than the person you eventually married? How serious were you? What happened to those relationships?*

_____

_____

_____

_____

_____

3. *How good were you at maintaining trust, love, care, and sharing in your close friendships?*

_____

_____

_____

_____

_____

_____

4. *How did you handle disagreements when they cropped up? How well did you negotiate and compromise? Explain.*

_____

_____

_____

_____

_____

5. *How well did you give mutual support and empathy to your most intimate relationship in your twenties? How well was this reciprocated? Explain.*

_____

_____

_____

_____

_____

"Our twenties are filled with establishing social networks different and more substantial than those in our teens."

Self Life Arena

The theme of our twenties in this arena is one of achieving autonomy and an adult identity uniquely our own. Naturally, we will continue to define this identity, search for personal values, and explore our expanding self-concepts. We put together our own world-view and develop our own points of view, all of which we continuously clarify. We develop support systems for our emotional, mental, and psychological health. Balancing all of our growing interests—which vie for more and more of our time and energy—becomes a priority for the first time. The skills of problem solving, time management, stress management, and change management are all parts of the curriculum of this arena in this decade of life.

1. How did your self-concept change during these ten years? Describe.

_____

_____

_____

_____

_____

2. What kind of changes occurred during this time in your view of yourself? Explain.

_____

_____

_____

_____

3. How did you handle the changes that were going on in your life during this time? What was your problem solving style or mode? Give examples.

_____

_____

_____

_____

_____

4. How well did you handle criticism or rejection? Does it differ from how you handle criticism today?

_____

_____

_____

_____

_____

_____

5. What physical attribute or ability did your appreciate most about yourself during this decade? Describe.

_____

_____

_____

_____

_____

"The theme of our twenties in this arena is one of achieving autonomy and an adult identity uniquely our own."

Leisure Life Arena

As with the other arenas of this decade, your leisure life arena involved much exploration. The strength, resources, mobility, and maturity to bring your childhood fantasies into reality was found here. You could now "climb mountains," run races, read any book you desired, and learn whatever you wanted. You were your own person, had freedom, health, and energy—you were on top of the world. Your horizons had been considerably broadened and you could, for the first time perhaps, exploit these options and opportunities with vigor.

1. Did you realize any of your childhood fantasies during this time? Did you travel to a tropical island? climb Mount Everest? play for a major league sports team? What? Describe and explain.

2. What new leisure interests did you engage in? Describe.

3. What forms of entertainment did you favor during this time? Describe and explain.

4. What part of your leisure time was actually recuperative rest from working? To what degree did you enjoy fun purely for its own sake?

5. What kinds of cars did you own or operate during these years? To what degree did you enjoy them? Describe, using examples.

"The strength, resources, mobility, and maturity to bring your childhood fantasies into reality was found here."

Spirit Life Arena

Our spiritual life during this decade is characterized by an urge to stabilize the spiritual turmoil of our teens. We search for a surer philosophy of life that we can actually put into practice in our daily lives. Doubts are still with us, but they may not shake us like they did earlier. Since we are now confronted with living in an adult world, we are forced to solidify our basic value system and decide on pragmatic "rights" and "wrongs." We are so much "in the world" during this decade that it's hard to focus on the fact that we are not "of the world." Still, we do feel close to God in ways too diffuse for words: We know that God is there through it all, but life is so busy and the possibilities of the future are so compelling that we may find it difficult to focus on the spiritual dimension.

1. *Did you experience any personal crises of belief during this time? Did your faith help you handle them?*

2. *Who was your principal spiritual guide or model? Explain.*

3. *Describe your concept of God during this time in your life. What kind of personal relationship did your have with God?*

4. *Describe your most personal and meaningful events and relationships during these years.*

5. *For what did you pray during your twenties? Describe.*

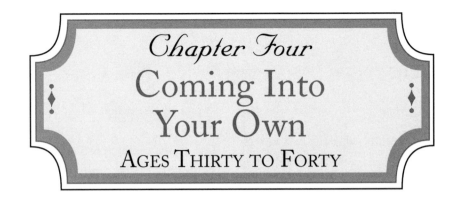

My fourth decade began on my thirtieth birthday: _____.

Significant historical events of this ten-year-period were:

_____

_____

_____

_____

_____

In our thirties, we begin to take stock, and thus come to see ourselves more clearly. We realize a deeper dimension of independence where we may find new hope well beyond anything we have formerly experienced. The busyness of our thirties, however, may prevent us from taking the time to adequately do the spiritual homework necessary to surmount the challenges of personal development. The busyness can so distract us that we fail to learn the dramatic life lessons of this time. Consequently, we are at risk of robbing ourselves of the gentle yet powerful feeling of knowing that we are meeting the challenges of living, and have found a psychospiritual place of peace.

When we can't find a sense of security inside, we seek external supports to provide us with some semblance of hope. Feeling inadequate inside, we begin to look to others for the confidence we can't seem to muster from within. In the busyness of pursuing worldly success, we can lose our internal sense of God's centering presence, and become dependent on others and things outside of ourselves. We roam about, as it were, frantically turning over every stone in search for that person, medicine, or formula which will give us some relief from feeling so insecure. These outside supports are insufficient, of course, and so we live in fear that they will evaporate and leave us "hanging" without any assurance that tomorrow will turn out well.

If this fear intensifies, as it can in our frantic thirties, we run the risk of entering into the inevitable next phase of dependency: despondency. Developmental despondency, a condition just shy of despair, is the precursor to hopelessness. We can feel forlorn, inadequate, sad, blue, depressed; any sense of direction or purpose evades us. Developmental despondency strips us of the noble

assurance that the power of love is the mightiest force in the world. We feel stuck in a circular path leading nowhere.

Certainly, not everyone in their thirties experiences such a despondency, yet the risk of falling into an ennui, or personal angst, just this side of depression is a very real one. We strive for connection, for commun-ion; yet, some succumb to the "fake" of the world and look for this connection in the physical world alone. We move into "more-living" and "when-living": "I'll be happier, if I have 'more,'" and " I'll be happier, 'when…'!" The degree to which this attitude prevails is the degree to which it clouds our spiritual growth and develop-ment.

School/Career/Work Life Arena

"Making it" in the world, however we each define that, becomes the consuming thrust of the thirties in the career life arena. We have moved out of the exploration stage and are working hard to establish ourselves. Whether by climbing the career ladder or running the best household that we can, we seek to become all that we feel we should become. We struggle to achieve mastery in so many ways: we may seek more education or training; we adjust to the realities of working in situations that might not "fit" our own life dream; we commit our work identities to a path which sets a pattern for the decade; we try to solidify our career goals; we seek confidence, credentials, recognition, ways of making contributions, and many other things in our attempts to becoming our own person.

1. Describe your career path during this time. Was it disjointed or steady? Explain.

_____

_____

_____

_____

_____

2. Did you always like your work during this decade? Were there times when you would rather not have gone to work? Explain.

_____

_____

_____

3. Did you feel that you were "in charge" of your career? Were there persons, conditions, events, situations, etc. which hampered you? Explain.

_____

_____

_____

_____

_____

4. In what ways were you seeking or striving in your work during this time? What were your big work challenges? Explain.

_____

_____

_____

_____

_____

5. How confident were you in your work during this decade? To what degree did you feel like you were making a contribution to your community in this decade?

_____

_____

_____

Family Life Arena

People who study adult development say that it is around the age of thirty we come to a true, internal commitment to both work and love. As with career establishment—seeking security and mastery in one's work life—so is it in the family life arena. We further establish our parent role and our marriage partner role. With commitment comes an enhanced "staying power" in our marriage, and we seek deeper levels of mutuality, respect, communication, and trust. Putting down roots becomes more important, so we enhance and decorate our homes and gardens. House maintenance becomes more important; building secure happy homes for our families is the order of the day.

1. *What were the big issues in your family during this decade in your life? Explain.*

_____

_____

_____

_____

_____

2. *How well did you handle disciplining your children during this time in your life? Please give specifics.*

_____

_____

_____

_____

_____

3. *How was the responsibility and division of labor decided in your family? Explain, giving some examples.*

_____

_____

_____

_____

_____

4. *How did it feel to watch your children grow up? Explain, using as many details as possible.*

_____

_____

_____

_____

_____

_____

5. *To what degree did you interact with your own parents during this decade of your life? How did your relationship with them change during this time?*

_____

_____

_____

_____

_____

"We further establish our parent role and our marriage partner role."

Relationship Life Arena

In our thirties, social contacts generally expand through work, community involvement, and, for parents, through contact with other parents, group leaders, and teachers. While some social networks are expanding, others might be decreasing. We are called to adjust to some friendships from earlier years that are becoming estranged; people move away, go in different directions, etc. We reappraise our longstanding relationships. As we change, and our more authentic self unfolds bit by bit, we learn new ways of relating to others as well. We attempt to integrate our lives as much as possible, and our friendships are a logical avenue for this task.

1. *Who made up your circle of friends during this decade? How strong a social support network did they provide for you?*

_____

_____

_____

_____

_____

2. *Did you have persons with whom you could share your innermost thoughts and feelings? Were these relationships satisfying for you? Give specifics.*

_____

_____

_____

_____

_____

3. *To what degree did you feel you were loved and cared for? Whom did this love and care come from? Explain.*

_____

_____

_____

_____

_____

4. *Relate several memorable events you shared with friends during this decade of your life.*

_____

_____

_____

_____

_____

5. *Were you more of a "giver" or a "taker" in your close relationships? Give specific examples.*

_____

_____

_____

_____

_____

Self Life Arena

The quest for personal autonomy is felt most acutely here in the inner life arena. The big questions, "Who am I, really?" and "Where am I going?" continue their itching deep inside. Yet the world of our thirties is a busy place which doesn't encourage extended periods of introspection; there's always more work to do! Life balance, deciding how to allocate our limited energy, becomes an increasing concern. We are continuously adapting and integrating our sense of self, our self-definition. Health maintenance becomes a more central concern as the first signs of aging begin to peek through our youthfulness. We crave more time for ourselves, more time for thinking, more time for just "being" instead of always "doing."

1. *To what degree did you feel independent and autonomous in your personal life during this decade? Explain.*

_____

_____

_____

_____

_____

2. *What were your highest priorities? Try to name them in order of their importance to you.*

_____

_____

_____

3. *Did you like yourself during this time in your life? Explain.*

_____

_____

_____

_____

_____

_____

_____

4. *How did you see yourself expanding during this decade? Explain.*

_____

_____

_____

_____

_____

5. *What were some of the big personal issues or even problems which required your attention and solution? Explain.*

_____

_____

_____

_____

Leisure Life Arena

Demands from the other arenas mandated some dramatic concessions of our leisure during this decade, causing us to change the activities and patterns we had established in the previous decade. Our leisure became less physical and more socially oriented. Feeling a loss in this, we may have experimented with new leisure goals which required some training, practice, adventure, and travel. We missed the more active lifestyle of the previous decade and became increasingly aware of the need for more physical activity, not simply for the fun and competition of it, but for its health promotion aspects. Like every other arena, our leisure was changing as well.

1. *How did your leisure time change in this decade as compared to the previous one? Explain.*

_____

_____

_____

_____

2. *Summing it up in a few words, what was your philosophy of leisure during this decade?*

_____

_____

_____

_____

_____

3. *Who were your favorite movie stars/sports figures? Describe.*

_____

_____

_____

_____

_____

_____

4. *Did you try any new leisure pursuits that may not have been very successful? Explain.*

_____

_____

_____

_____

_____

_____

5. *What were your favorite "play things" during this decade? Describe.*

_____

_____

_____

_____

_____

"Demands from the other arenas mandated some dramatic concessions of our leisure during this decade, causing us to change the activities and patterns we had established in the previous decade."

Spirit Life Arena

Unless there was a significant personal crisis during this decade, the growth in this arena is more subliminal than obvious. We have needs for expressing our spirituality, but the personal spiritual search is usually not ignited until events or changes push us to our spiritual edge. We pray for balance and harmony, for our children, and for the world. Seldom do we pray for ourselves in this decade. We know that God is there, but we are not often moved by any spiritual crisis or confounding doubts that motivate us to get closer to God. We remain outwardly focused, we are still very much "in" the world.

1. *What kind of spiritual or inner perspective did you feel in these years?*

_____

_____

_____

_____

_____

2. *How did you generally practice your spiritual leanings during this time? Explain.*

_____

_____

_____

_____

_____

3. *To what degree did you feel spiritually "in touch" with God during this decade? Explain.*

_____

_____

_____

_____

_____

4. *Did you experience any spiritual crises or doubts? Describe your feelings as best you can.*

_____

_____

_____

_____

_____

5. *What were your most fulfilling joys and blessings of this decade? Describe.*

_____

_____

_____

_____

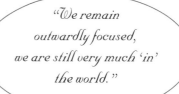

"We remain outwardly focused, we are still very much 'in' the world."

Chapter Five
Hitting the Wall
AGES FORTY TO FIFTY

This decade began for me on _____.

Some of the most memorable world events of my forties were:

_____

_____

_____

_____

_____

Our forties serve as a developmental bridge between the first and second half of our lives. Just as the first decade of our lives lays down the foundation for the first half of our life, so the decade of our forties lays down the foundation for the second half.

In this marvelous yet tumultuous decade we come to understand ourselves in ways quite different from before. We enter our forties feeling perhaps more confident than we ever did, almost cocky. We leave our forties wondering how we could ever feel so complacent. In-between these two points, we feel growth pangs of development that will reverberate the rest of our lives. What are some of these growth pangs?

1. Loss of youth. For the first time, we realize that we may have less time to live than we have already lived. This realization sends shock waves through us which motivate reactions of many different dimensions. Divorce rates jump in the forties, the so-called midlife crisis rattles many of us, teenage children introduce a sometimes exasperating element into our lives, job changes, increasing aging of our own parents…all of these show us various facets of our loss of youth.

2. Brokenness. In our forties, we look at the brokenness many of us experienced in our youthful excesses. We also develop a level of maturity that enables us to view ourselves as fallible; before this, we seemed to use our relative youth as an excuse for our transgressions, thinking we had plenty of time to live another life.

3. Shift in the meaning of time. Time, formerly unendingly abundant, now has limits. We find a more conservative tendency creeping into our overall

perspective. A new sense of urgency emerges because time is now exhaustible.

4. Stock-taking. With the change occurring all around, we quite naturally begin to look back and ask: "How have I done in life so far?" This seemingly innocent question sparks an ever growing sense of personal history. We realize, in an ever more profound way, that we "have a history." This statement of personal substance propels us to begin a process which will be with us till the end of our days: taking stock in our lives…life review.

5. New attitude toward God. As with everything else, our view of God shifts as well. We recognize that the God of our youth is changing from an ever-benevolent yet impersonal God who saved me from harm into a much more personal God who resides in me and allows me to "handle" the inevitable challenges of life.

6. Disillusionment. Our forties, with its sometimes wrenching self-reflection, make us ask for more meaning from life than simply worldly success. We look more deeply into our work and seek therein a broader sense of self, an arena not only to accomplish things, but a forum where we can better express our authentic self.

7. New definition of self. Old self-definitions seem inadequate as we progress through our forties. The previous decades somehow seemed more structured than the present; a new and hauntingly vague uneasiness creeps into our lives in our forties. This seems paradoxical because, at the same time, we see that we have become more confident with things of the world than ever before, yet strangely insecure at the same time.

Career/Work Life Arena

Somewhere in this decade, we confront ourselves as never before in this arena. We have harvested enough personal history to look back and gain a more focused perspective. We look at our earlier career dream and compare it to the reality of our current work life. We ask ourselves: "Is this what I had planned? Is this what I wanted?" The entire decade is consumed with such questions. Our response will determine whether we move toward career renewal or career resignation. We seek adjustment in our "dream," and move toward compromise as well as reestablishment of a new dream tempered by the fray of reality.

1. *During these years did you feel you were fulfilling the "dream" you had for your life as it related to your work? Explain.*

2. *Did your experience any fundamental changes in the "meaning of work"—or related to your work role—in these "middle years"?*

3. *What would you say were your most successful work accomplishments during this period? Describe.*

4. *Describe the kind of work you performed during this decade. What new skills did you learn?*

5. *What work-related promotions did you receive (or give to yourself)? Describe.*

"We seek adjustment in our 'dream,' and move toward compromise as well as reestablishment of a new dream tempered by the fray of reality."

Family Life Arena

Many forces are swirling in this arena as well. The family usually enters the age where children become teenagers. This is potentially the most stressful time for parenting; our little ones are growing bigger, but they think they have become young adults. Our culture pushes premature maturation which can clash with our wishes as parents. Our children don't need the same kind of parental care as before, but the care they do need can challenge and frustrate us as never before. We also realize, perhaps for the first time, that our own parents are aging and will need help soon. This leaves both a burden and an opportunity at our doorstep. Our marriage (if we are married) is haunted by new pressures which take much of our energy.

1. *To what degree was this a time of marital or familial readjustment? Describe.*

_____

_____

_____

_____

2. *Explain some of the "putting-down-roots" activities or experiences in your family during this decade.*

_____

_____

_____

_____

_____

3. *Describe experiences of relating to your teenage children. Try to recall specific incidents.*

_____

_____

_____

_____

_____

4. *What changes took place in your relationship with your parents during this time? What were your feelings?*

_____

_____

_____

_____

_____

5. *Describe some memorable situations and/or circumstances from your family life that you recall from this decade.*

_____

_____

_____

_____

Relationship Life Arena

In the so-called "middle years," we look to our relationships in a different way and find either deepened intimacy or its opposite in them. We ask for more and different things from our relationships than we did in the past. The stress of the changes taking place make us rely on our relationships more heavily, which means that our relationships will either rise to the occasion or buckle under the changes. It's a time for reevaluating and reasserting our commitment to our relationships. We seek a deeper sense of communication, a sharing on a much more mature level that will lead to a new sense of mutuality or togetherness as a result of a shared relationship of respect. In our friendships, too, we seek a new sharing at greater depths; rather than seeking simply communication, we seek communion.

1. *Did you deepen your social involvement or broaden your circle of friends during this period? If so (or not), explain.*

2. *How did your relationships change with friends or "special people" during this time in your life? Explain.*

3. *Was it easy or difficult in your marital/intimate relationship to allow each other room for a sense of independence?*

4. *How would you characterize your most intimate relationship during this period? Did you make any changes? Were there changes that you wanted to make? Explain.*

5. *Relate several memorable experiences you shared with your friends and/or your spouse during this decade.*

Self Life Arena

Perhaps the most far-reaching change in the self life arena at this time is in the perspective of time. We are normally confronted with a life changing realization: we have already lived more time than we can count on having left. This new view of time first sends ripples of uncertainty, and then a nervous sense of urgency, through us. We try to get "in touch" with our original dreams and assess how and whether life has lived up to them. This reassessment pushes us to make changes like never before. In the end, we either find new life through renewal or we resign ourselves to our "old" life predicament. The midlife crisis can be very real, and very painful!

1. *Do you feel that this was a broadening and enhancing period for you or a solidifying and stabilizing one? Explain.*

_____

_____

_____

_____

_____

2. *Did you become more or less opinionated in your thinking during this decade? Explain.*

_____

_____

_____

_____

3. *Were you more inclined to push your energy outward or inward toward self-development, meditation, introspection, etc.?*

_____

_____

_____

_____

_____

4. *How important was the maintenance of your body and health during this decade? What specific things did you do to help you in this endeavor? Explain.*

_____

_____

_____

_____

_____

_____

5. *What was your greatest personal success during this decade? Describe.*

_____

_____

_____

_____

"We are normally confronted with a life changing realization: we have already lived more time than we can count on having left."

Leisure Life Arena

In this decade, leisure interests and activities generally shift. In previous decades, we engaged more in endeavors where we exerted our bodies. As we approach fifty, we usually slow down a bit and shift our leisure more toward sedentary and social endeavors. This is not exclusive, of course, just a tendency. We begin using our leisure time for greater personal expansion: Intellectual pursuits, like reading or card playing while socializing, are examples of this shift. We see leisure more as a stress-reducing diversion than a physical outlet. It's not so much changing the specific activities that are changing, it's more a reshuffle of the mix.

1. *Did you establish any new leisure goals or "dreams" during this ten-year-period in your life? Explain.*

_____

_____

_____

_____

_____

2. *Who did you primarily spend your leisure time with during this decade? Describe and explain why this was so.*

_____

_____

_____

_____

3. *Did you experience any decline in physical activity during this decade? How did these changes affect you? Explain.*

_____

_____

_____

_____

_____

4. *Did you get both mental and physical rest during this time in your life? Explain.*

_____

_____

_____

_____

5. *Describe any vacations and/or traveling you enjoyed in those years. How did these experiences affect you? Explain.*

_____

_____

_____

_____

"As we approach fifty, we usually slow down a bit and shift our leisure more toward sedentary and social endeavors. "

Spirit Life Arena

This arena generally takes on a heightened significance in the middle years. With the shift in time perspective, we become much more interested in the "big" questions of life, "What is God like?", "How do I get to heaven?", "What will be my fate?", "Have I been a good Christian?", and the like. We seek answers by reading, listening more closely to the weekly sermon, and by paying more attention to issues related to religion. In general, our interest and search for transpersonal issues intensifies and becomes much more serious. Spirituality becomes personally relevant as never before.

1. *How would you characterize your commitment to God—and the spiritual life—during this decade? Explain.*

_____

_____

_____

_____

_____

2. *Did you involve yourself in any spiritual training or Bible study during this time? How did this affect you spiritually? Explain.*

_____

_____

_____

_____

_____

3. *How and to whom did you share your spiritual ideas and questions?*

_____

_____

_____

_____

_____

4. *If your life during these years was a poem, what would be its title? Describe and explain.*

_____

_____

_____

_____

_____

5. *For what did you pray during this time in your life? Explain.*

_____

_____

_____

_____

_____

"Spirituality becomes personally relevant as never before."

Chapter Six
Laying a New Foundation
AGES FIFTY TO SIXTY

My sixth decade began on my fiftieth birthday: _____.

Several significant historical events of this decade were:

_____

_____

_____

_____

_____

In our fifties, the desire to make sense of our lives intensifies. Forces converge, offering the opportunity of a new perspective on how God has been at work in us all our days. We begin to discover the patterns, themes, successes, and failures that make up the unique experience that is our life. In this decade, we grow to see ourselves more clearly so we can do the work required to become the self we truly are.

In this decade, we revisit and redefine the difficult places and times that we knew were hard when we went through them. They now take on a new significance as we look back and reexperience them in the light of what has occurred since. We also begin to see new themes, stands, and waves that we formerly missed in the hectic environment of day-to-day living. Having gained the depth perception necessary to pause and come to a new understanding of what we may have overlooked before, we gain a fuller appreciation of the true meaning of the experience.

This new perspective sharpens our vision and gives our lives greater detail. We are able to raze or redesign some attitudes, values, and beliefs that may have outlived their usefulness. Not only that, we are pressed to unlearn much of what we have come to accept about the world and about ourselves in order to make room for a self that is less dependent on the world and more on God. This is the central spiritual task of the second half of our lives.

One of the things we realize at this point is that we have many stories to tell. We begin to perceive a generous history of life in ourselves. We find ourselves intrigued by it, and, whether we revel in it or we run away from it, we are captivated by it in some previously unknown way. With enhanced insight and perspective, we find more of ourselves in this personal story that is us.

Career/Work Life Arena

Our fifties usher in a period of settling down from the tumult of our forties. There are still challenges, however. We may feel the pressure of the skills, competitive spirit, energy, and drive of younger workers. We may respond to this pressure by emotionally resigning ourselves to "putting in time" until retirement, but it could also catapult us into the role of mentor. We feel an obligation to keep things going, to pass on our hard-earned lessons to those who will listen, and, in the process, the new mentor is personally enriched in the exchange. Certainly, we feel our advancing years. Persons we consider peers are making final retirement plans. This realization is shocking for some who may invest themselves all the more in their work. For others, the realization opens a door to greater personal and spiritual growth.

1. *To what degree were you invested in your work during this decade? Were there periods of feeling that you were just "putting in time"?*

2. *What was your biggest career disappointment/success during this decade? Describe each in detail.*

3. *What were your thoughts about retirement during this phase of your life? Did they change over this decade? Explain.*

4. *Were there certain person(s) for whom you served as a mentor during this period of your career? Explain.*

5. *Which aspects of your job did you like most/least during this time in your life? Describe.*

Family Life Arena

This is the "launching pad" decade for most families: It is the time when children leave to establish themselves. The frenzy of this is followed by the so-called "empty nest" syndrome of feeling a sense of loss combined with a sense of relief. We reconcile these changes within us by reinvesting ourselves in other family-related issues, such as home-care, grandparenting, elder caregiving, financial security, cooking, or gardening. We begin to taste the first sweetness of becoming the mentor or elder of the family; naturally, this role will only intensify as the years roll on.

1. *What was it like to be a parent of adult children? How did you, and they, cope with this new role?*

_____

_____

_____

_____

_____

2. *Describe how your children left home to start their own individual lives. What kind of impact did their leaving have upon the household?*

_____

_____

_____

_____

3. *How did you feel about your own parents aging? Describe.*

_____

_____

_____

_____

_____

4. *What might have been some changes in the way you cared for and maintained your home during this decade?*

_____

_____

_____

_____

_____

5. *Describe several memorable family events from this decade. How would you describe the atmosphere/ level of communication in the family as compared to previous times?*

_____

_____

_____

_____

"We begin to taste the first sweetness of becoming the mentor or elder of the family; naturally, this role will only intensify as the years roll on."

Relationship Life Arena

This can be a wonderful decade in our relationships. We develop a new comfort and mature calmness about our relationships. With increasing personal integration, our ego needs have sufficiently waned to allow the emergence of a more comfortable intimacy. Honest sharing becomes the primary theme of our relationships. We refine our relationships: those which offer greater intimacy are nurtured, while those relationships which lack this dimension slowly extinguish. We generally experience a heightened need for deeper sharing and a confidant—spouse, close friend, spiritual director, personal counselor—during this time, a person with whom we can share everything about our lives. If we fail in establishing a deeper intimate association, we may begin a slight drift toward social and personal isolation.

1. *In what ways did your circle of friends and emotional supports change during this time?*

2. *Who was the most memorable person for you during this decade? the most influential? the most caring?*

3. *In what ways did you experience loneliness during this decade? Describe and explain.*

4. *Did you care for your friends during this decade? With which of their needs were you most helpful? Explain.*

5. *Describe how your relationship with your spouse (special person) developed during this decade.*

"We develop a new comfort and mature calmness about our relationships."

Self Life Arena

While seeking greater intimacy in our relationships, we seek increased autonomy in the self arena. These paradoxical goals demonstrate the heightened need for personal integration we experience in our fifties. We continue the quest for an authentic self. Finding authenticity and uncovering integration means that we continuously deal with our inner contradictions: we love and fear at the same time, we seek wisdom and yet feel inadequate, we are propelled by mercy while compelled by indifference. Such contradictions used to frustrate us, but now we gradually let go of our tendency to need absolute consistency in our beliefs, perceptions, and thinking. Our fifties make us less compulsive and more caring in the fullest sense.

1. *What was your energy level during this decade? How did you use your energy in your self life arena?*

2. *In what ways did you change your life goals during this decade? Explain.*

3. *How did your body change during this decade? What did you think of these changes? Explain.*

4. *How did you attempt to maintain a positive attitude toward life during this time? Explain.*

5. *What were the most profound lessons about life you learned during this decade? Describe.*

"Our fifties make us less compulsive and more caring in the fullest sense."

Leisure Life Arena

In general, we have more time available for leisure activities. We continue to modify our leisure activities toward more mental and social activities, yet leisure in developing a new facet of potential brilliance begins to take on a personally fulfilling dimension of serenity. We seek inspiration, harmony, peace, and quiet in our leisure. To be sure, the "fun" aspects of leisure are still exciting, but the balance between leisure for "fun" and leisure for increased personal meaning is shifting. We may become more introspective, more thoughtful, and more respectful of the time we have been given. We renew ourselves with the restorative power of leisure.

1. In what ways might you have deepened your social involvement through your leisure at this time? Describe.

_____

_____

_____

_____

_____

2. How did you spend your leisure time during this decade?

_____

_____

_____

_____

3. To what degree did you allow yourself to enjoy rest and even idleness? Describe your feelings about this.

_____

_____

_____

_____

_____

_____

_____

4. What type of leisure travel did you pursue?

_____

_____

_____

_____

5. What personal satisfaction did you derive from your leisure life during this decade?

_____

_____

_____

"We renew ourselves with the restorative power of leisure."

_____

Spirit Life Arena

After the spiritual shock waves of our forties, a shift generally occurs in this decade toward an evolving of spiritual thinking and centering in a more steady, sustained relationship with God. Our prayer life becomes more focused, we invest in the study of spirituality, and church can become more central in our lives. We notice an evolving spiritual power, trust, and renewed respect for things spiritual. This may also be a time of spiritual unrest, especially if a crisis disrupts our routines: a physical sickness, an accident, an untimely death of a sibling can thrust us into spiritual turmoil. As death becomes more proximate in our lives, we quite naturally seek ways of reconciling the starkness of death with the vibrancy of our lives. Each of us works this out in his or her own ways.

1. Did you feel close to God during this decade? To what degree did you regard God as a real and sustaining force?

2. Describe your prayer life during this time in your life. What did you pray for?

3. How satisfying and meaningful was your spiritual life during this decade? Explain.

4. How did you react to death during this decade? Explain, using specifics if you can.

5. What was your most creative accomplishment of this decade? most beautiful experience? most surprising experience?

Chapter Seven
Finding New Drive
AGES SIXTY TO SEVENTY

This decade began on my sixtieth birthday: _____.

Significant historical events which occurred during this ten-year time frame that impacted on me were:

_____

_____

_____

_____

_____

The overriding theme of this decade is retirement. Whether retiring earlier than sixty or still actively working beyond seventy, we nonetheless encounter thundering changes related to work and work cessation. The average *first* retirement age in America is around fifty-eight; the average final retirement age (beyond which all paid work ceases) is sixty-three-and-a-half. The question of what to do with this new time takes central stage in our sixties. Retirement, of course, is defined differently by each and every person who enters into it. It no longer means a sedentary lifestyle (if it ever did); rather, retirement becomes a new forum for finding meaning, fulfillment, and purpose. Retirement is a time of renewal, refinement, reassessment, realignment, and rebalancing. Retirement affects every other arena in profound ways.

The second theme of this decade is that of grandparenting or surrogate grandparenting. A new generation populates our families, and we all gladly make room for them. Grandparents need contact with their grandchildren, and grandchildren need meaningful sharing with their grandparents. The grandparent/grandchild relationship is special. Grandparents can offer their grandchildren so much in terms of emotional grounding, family history, knowledge of the world, and an invaluable understanding of the maturation process. Grandchildren offer their grandparents an equal amount: proof that they are leaving a lasting legacy in the grandchildren themselves, a life purpose along with consequent expanded life meaning, the security of knowing that things are unfolding as they should in the world, and the rejuvenation of truly sharing their

wisdom with someone as important as their grand-child.

Yet in our culture, barriers have emerged which can confound the grandparent/grandchild relationship. Geographic estrangement—grandparents and grand-children living at great distances from each other—which severely reduces the opportunity for meaningful contact, is an increasing problem; and the desire for a retirement lifestyle in a warm climate can rob both grandparent and grandchild of the proximity that may have been present in years past when affluence was not as comprehensive and retirement options were not as broad. A fast-paced lifestyle for both the grandparent and grandchild also hampers opportunities for sharing communication and connectedness. Ingrained ageism, a prejudice against older persons, is unfortunately quite pervasive in our culture. Grandchildren, especially teen-agers, may suffer some embarrassment about being with their own grandparents. Conversely, grandparents may feel somewhat inhibited from genuinely sharing them-selves with their grandchildren because they may feel the sting of ageism in other corners of the culture which have somehow reduced their sense of self.

These factors by no means affect all grandparents and grandchildren, yet there are few grandparents who would deny that they wish for a closer and deeper rela-tionship with their grandchildren in some ways. The fact is that we need to encourage intergenerational con-nectedness as much as we can. Grandchildren need to gain respect for their grandparents as models of a mature life that is peaceful, agreeable, gentle, caring, and wise without being the least bit overbearing. The grandparent needs to perceive the grandchild as good, healthy, fun, capable of loving—and needs to do all of this without criticism. This is no small trick!

One of the ways grandparents and grandchildren can accomplish deeper connectedness is through sharing their respective stories. Both grandparents and grand-children can become consummate storytellers if each gives the other permission to proceed, and this permis-sion is buttressed by genuine interest in the ongoing welfare of each other. Storytelling remains a premier way for the generations to pass down cultural and familial information and wisdom, and the best stories are the personal ones. It is through the unfolding of the story that intimacy flowers, empathetic identification grows, and strong, lasting bonds take hold. But stories can become boring if they are redundant, or if they con-tain a personal "axe to grind." Clear communication skills need to be modeled by the elder partner in the intergenerational pair.

Career/Work Life Arena

Preparation for retirement consumes the career/ work life arena in this decade. We live in a culture that encourages us to define ourselves by our work. When time comes for disengaging from this lifestyle, we are required to redefine the person we have been for so long. This is no easy process. We are compelled to reassess our worth, finances, sources of happiness, health, purpose, marriage or intimate relationships, responsibilities, aging, and even our very reason for being. This takes time, energy, insight, and lots of help. Many companies have preretirement programs, yet the deep-down inner life work, required for a thorough life discernment prior to retirement, is done on our own. It takes reading, reflection, discussions, and lots of thought to navigate the sometimes rocky paths to retirement success.

1. *How did you feel about the changes in your work life during this decade? Describe in detail.*

_____

_____

_____

_____

_____

2. *Describe anticipating your retirement (or that of your spouse) in terms of your innermost feelings and fears.*

_____

_____

_____

3. *Did you enjoy your work in this decade as much as or more than in previous ones?*

_____

_____

_____

_____

_____

4. *Describe any volunteer work, etc. that you did primarily for your own pleasure or fulfillment.*

_____

_____

_____

_____

_____

5. *What were your most successful work accomplishments during this decade? Describe.*

_____

_____

_____

_____

"Preparation for retirement consumes the career/work life arena in this decade."

Family Life Arena

With our own children usually having families of their own, the main accent of the family life arena generally is on the extended family. We focus on grandchildren, grandnieces, grandnephews, etc. We become caregivers, often to our adult children, our grandchildren, and even our aging parents—sometimes all at once. The caregiving role can provide tremendous meaning and joy, as well as lots of potential frustration. Care needs can sometimes stretch our resources beyond our ability to give. Yet on we go, doing what we can, while trying to accomplish our own growth goals at the same time.

1. *What changes occurred in your family during this decade? Describe thoroughly.*

_____

_____

_____

_____

_____

2. *What new roles of caring did you take on during this decade of your life?*

_____

_____

_____

_____

_____

_____

3. *What type of relationship did you foster with your grandchildren during this period?*

_____

_____

_____

_____

_____

_____

4. *What changes occurred in your own parents (if they were still alive) during this decade? How did you react to the death of family members?*

_____

_____

_____

_____

_____

_____

5. *What are the memorable events which stick out in your mind from this decade? How do you feel about these events now?*

_____

_____

_____

_____

_____

"Care needs can sometimes stretch our resources beyond our ability to give."

Relationship Life Arena

During this decade, healthy marriages move into a phase which can be called "honest, mature devotion," characterized by a gentle, caring, respectful, and peaceful companionship and sense of commitment. Naturally, this serenity can be punctuated by periods of contention as well, but we quickly bounce back. We are called to renew our involvement in relationships at church, as well as other community associations and organizations. We generally need to extend our social networks as we lose some of our friends to death or moves. We want to expand and deepen our personal relationships; our confidante(s) becomes more, not less, important. We seek sharing, yet we seek more solitude as well. Social interaction needs to remain strong lest we risk dipping into a loneliness and isolation which breeds emotional instability.

1. *Did you expand your interest in community affairs during this time?*

_____

_____

_____

_____

2. *Did you lose any close friends during this time? What was your reaction? Explain.*

_____

_____

_____

3. *Describe the changes that took place in your circle of friends during this decade.*

_____

_____

_____

_____

_____

4. *Did you find it easier or more difficult to express your true, genuine feelings to your friends and family during this period?*

_____

_____

_____

_____

_____

_____

5. *Were you more able and/or ready to forgive others (and yourself) during this decade? Did you become more accepting or more opinionated? Explain.*

_____

_____

_____

_____

_____

Self Life Arena

The search for our authentic self continues in this decade. We find that thoughts from the past cascade before our mind's eye more and more. Changes in our career arena ripple through the self arena: "Who am I now that I no longer have work to define me?", "What is my purpose in life now?", "How will I relate to others?", "How do I deal with my own aging?", "How can I value the present in my life?" These questions reverberate through our mind and provide either a foundation for renewal or the seeds for resignation. The Paschal Mystery of death to new life—of loss to gain—repeats itself over and over throughout life, yet it is in this decade we are faced with developing a deeper understanding of it.

1. *What were your emotional reactions to the role changes you experienced during this decade?*

_____

_____

_____

_____

_____

_____

2. *What changes occurred in your health and/or physical condition during this decade? Explain, using concrete examples.*

_____

_____

_____

_____

_____

3. *Did you notice any changes in your commitment or devotion to yourself, your goals, or a cause that was important to you in the past? Explain.*

_____

_____

_____

_____

_____

4. *What was your most prized possession during this period? What meaning did it have for you? Describe.*

_____

_____

_____

_____

_____

5. *What were your most memorable personal achievements during this decade? Describe.*

_____

_____

_____

_____

_____

Leisure Life Arena

It's in the leisure arena that we find some of the answers raised by our disengagement from the working years. Our involvement with leisure takes on a more robust status in our overall lifestyle in this decade. Leisure used to be what we did when we didn't *have* to do anything else; now, leisure is better defined as the source of physical rejuvenation, intellectual stimulation, and spiritual enrichment. Leisure is not simply diversionary activities, but rather a state of mind that helps us see the awe and wonder we may have overlooked in our working years. Now, we are free to learn new skills, new ideas, new attitudes. This freedom is spawned by our release from the confinement of work. However fulfilling work may have been for us in the past, this is a new day, and it's in our leisure arena where real personal growth can explode.

1. *Which leisure activities helped you fulfill the personal needs that were no longer being met at work? Explain.*

2. *What new leisure activity skills did you develop or discover during this period?*

3. *Did you search for activities that would prove satisfying or even exciting for you during this time? Describe.*

4. *To what degree did you feel creative in your leisure pursuits during this time? Explain.*

5. *What were the highlights of your leisure life? What did you enjoy the most and with whom? Describe.*

Spirit Life Arena

This arena rebounds almost as much as the leisure arena in this decade. We confront ourselves and find that our real identity is spiritual. Spiritual truths become clearer and more meaningful for us during this decade of our sixties. We find ourselves thinking more about God and eternity, the meaning of life, and its real joys. We appreciate things more and have deeper gratitude for all things. We see God where we used to see only shadows. A new and zest-filled panorama of spiritual energy is opened to those able to see what's really there in front of us. The inability to perceive this reality can make us critical and bitter, seeing the world merely as a place where we suffer loss, and where the aging process is the biggest thief.

1. *What was the most significant spiritual event you encountered during this time? Explain.*

2. *Did you feel close to God during this time in your life? Describe your feelings.*

3. *What changes did you notice in your faith during this decade?*

4. *Did it become easier or more difficult to perceive people as spiritual beings during this decade of your life? Explain.*

5. *If your life during these years was made into a movie, what would be its title? Explain.*

"We confront ourselves and find that our real identity is spiritual."

Chapter Eight
Developing a New Vision
AGE SEVENTY AND BEYOND

Our seventies bring the joy of enhanced personal integration, along with the stark fact that our bodies are beginning to let us down. Women seem much more adept at dealing with this physical diminishment than do men. Women are socialized to a nurturing role starting very early in their formative years. This role assists in providing a legitimate social role when they move into their later years by providing some health promoting mechanism. Men, by contrast, seem almost exclusively socialized (trained) to work. When the capacity for working is undercut by physical diminishments, the whole personality of the male can begin to unravel.

Our reactions and responses to physical diminishment will increasingly set the tone for our emotional health during this decade. If we can learn the purpose of our diminishments, however meager, then this decade can move along with an ageless growth and development not heretofore experienced. If we cannot, we will languish in a state of ennui, wishing that all this wasn't happening, and a cognitive depravity that life was better "back when."

Francis Dorff, O.Praem., coined the term "meditative writing." By this he means keeping a free-floating, private, daily journal of our innermost thoughts, feelings, and decisions. Writing "for our own eyes only" creates a meditative process where "some of the memories that come back to us we welcome wholeheartedly; others, we wish we had never remembered. Welcome or not, all of these experiences are part of our lives. When we remember them, it is often a sign that they now have something more to say to us" (op.cit., page 51).

Using a hyphen in "re-membering," Dorff denotes that the process of remembering is not simply bringing to mind events long past; rather, re-membering is to take these memories and fold them into our overall perspective in new ways. This process means that we use our memories to construct a much more integrative and holistic understanding of our past. Our memories may in fact be dis-membered, fragmented, and out-of-place. Writing about such memories allows us to consider them anew and to re-member them in a new context of our lives, a context that has the luxury and benefit of hindsight.

This memory reconstruction process pays rich dividends for us in terms of generating peace and purpose in our lives. The actual purpose of an event may have been clouded when it first occurred. In the new context of our seventies, we may see its true meaning shining through the clouds of former years.

As we move into our senior years, we gain the comfort of acceptance and a keener spiritual vision. What formerly seemed a wayward or unwanted act in the drama of our lives is now recognized as a true turning point that brought about wondrous growth that would otherwise be hidden from us. We realize the delightful irony that the "stone that was once rejected has become the cornerstone." This image becomes a metaphor for so much of what we considered tragedies or undesired clutter in our lives, but which now is recognized as a pivotal point in our development.

Career/Work Life Arena

As we move through our seventies and eighties, the distinctions between the six life arenas begins to blur. This is not some pathologic process; rather, this is the result of our becoming increasingly integrated. In the arena of career/work, we may encounter a shadow of fear, as finding direction becomes a challenge in this time of life. When the perspective of work is gone, we seek to replace what was lost. We may find ourselves longing for former times, or at least thinking that "I was better back when!" Such a thought process is regressive—it fixates on the past rather than seeing today as a forum for growth.

1. *What changes are evolving in your sense of competition in this phase of your life? Explain, using examples where possible.*

_____

_____

_____

_____

_____

2. *What kinds of skills are you learning that can be related, even indirectly, to an occupation past or present? Explain.*

_____

_____

_____

_____

3. *Describe what it is like to be retired. Try to be as specific as possible.*

_____

_____

_____

_____

_____

4. *What is your evaluation of your entire work life as you look back over it? What aspects might you wish had been different? Explain and give details.*

_____

_____

_____

_____

_____

5. *What do you consider your most successful work-related accomplishments? Describe.*

_____

_____

_____

_____

_____

"When the perspective of work is gone, we seek to replace what was lost."

Family Life Arena

This arena demands much change at this time. We may be called to adjust to the loss of a mate. The emotional, financial, and physical consequences of this shock us. We may have to live a single lifestyle, shift residence, and adjust to reduced income. This time of life may usher in the necessity of becoming a recipient of care rather than the caregiver. Such a reversal demands that we accept, tolerate, and love in ways vastly different than before. We relate to our married/adult children differently. At times we may feel uncomfortable with this new family arrangement, yet we find ourselves increasingly dependent on our children and/or others. We may even develop a surrogate family: neighbors and/or caregivers may become "like family" for us. This is another new dimension of family, one that is on the rise today.

1. *What is it like to lose your marital partner (or very close friend)? Describe your feelings.*

_____

_____

_____

_____

_____

2. *Describe the adjustment to living as a single person, if this has occurred.*

_____

_____

_____

_____

3. *How do you feel toward the people who help you during this stage of life?*

_____

_____

_____

_____

_____

4. *How would you describe your relationship with grandchildren, grandnieces, or grandnephews? What do you wish for them? Describe.*

_____

_____

_____

_____

_____

5. *Are you able to do as much for your family now as you did previously? How are your abilities and resources in this area changing? Describe.*

_____

_____

_____

_____

_____

Relationship Life Arena

Even though a sizeable percentage of married couples lose their spouse during this time, the need for companionship and social relationships does not cease; more than ever, we need to share ourselves with others and to see God in the eyes of others. There is a healing and uplifting element in staying close to others—alienation breeds sickness in us. We work to maintain current relationships and also to build new ones. The competencies of making and keeping friends becomes ever more important. We work to extend ourselves into the surrounding community and to stay interested in others. We participate in church and community groups, and enjoy the company of others. We seek to help in any ways we can. We keep "in touch."

1. *What changes in your social circle are you experiencing at this time? Describe.*

_____

_____

_____

_____

_____

2. *How would you compare this time in your life with your adolescent years regarding the type and depth of friendships? Explain.*

_____

_____

_____

_____

3. *What changes, if any, do you notice in your general level of caring and empathy as compared to previous decades? Explain.*

_____

_____

_____

_____

_____

_____

4. *What experiences of loneliness challenge you now? Describe.*

_____

_____

_____

_____

_____

_____

5. *Relate several memorable events you have shared with friends or special persons during this time in your life. Describe.*

_____

_____

_____

_____

_____

_____

Self Life Arena

Perhaps the biggest challenge in the self life arena at this stage is adaptability. Adaptability is being able to conform to the necessities of living, taking on the challenges that confront us rather than resisting them, and converting ourselves in response, rather than reacting to the changes that life brings. It's harmonizing with the ongoing flow of life rather than denying or becoming submissive to it. In short, it's adjusting to being in this world but realizing ever more clearly that we are not of this world. All this adaptation requires strength, patience, steadfastness, and courage—the building blocks for ongoing faith development.

1. *Are you able to affirm or even strengthen your personal independence in this time of your life? Explain.*

_____

_____

_____

_____

_____

_____

2. *List some of the changes you experience now in your thoughts about yourself as compared to previous times.*

_____

_____

_____

_____

_____

3. *Describe the level of health you enjoy. How do you feel about your health as compared to earlier?*

_____

_____

_____

_____

_____

_____

4. *How would you describe your level of self-confidence? Explain.*

_____

_____

_____

_____

_____

_____

5. *Do you have more or fewer problems living at this time as compared to previous decades? Describe.*

_____

_____

_____

_____

"Perhaps the biggest challenge in the self life arena at this stage is adaptability."

Leisure Life Arena

Leisure also requires more focus for us now, but it must remain a diversion from our main purpose in life. We recognize more clearly our leisure needs, including a contemplative bent. This insight lets us see God's creation as a celebration of what it genuinely is. Leisure bears many gifts in this time of living: motivation, socialization, self-confidence, relaxation, creativity, exercise, and entertainment. Leisure gives us the perspective of gratefulness, serenity, simplicity, acceptance, and patience. Leisure allows us to appreciate the present moment as one full of miracles, pregnant with God's love. When elevated to the spiritual level, leisure has the power to fill us with delight. We can transcend the physical plane and enter the holy playground of God's omnipresent joy.

1. *What new leisure interests have you learned in the past five years or so? Describe.*

2. *To what degree can you enjoy fun for its own sake? Does your response differ from what it would have been fifty years ago?*

3. *Describe your social leisure at this time. What changes, if any, would you like to make?*

4. *What level of meaning, satisfaction, and joy do you derive from your leisure pursuits? Explain.*

5. *Of all the leisure activities in your life, which are most memorable to you? Describe.*

"When elevated to the spiritual level, leisure has the power to fill us with delight."

Spirit Life Arena

Our spiritual lives are advancing with gusto at this time in life. The maturation process brings many losses which call us to mourning. Yet, mourning need not be a veil of tears, a depressed affect, or a sorrowful countenance. On the contrary, spiritual mourning leads us to the promise of God's joy and life in abundance. Love *is* all around us, and we can see it when we relinquish our need for a world where all is "right." We can come to see the world, and all that is in it, as a lesson to rely on God's power and grace as we confidently deal with the pain of the world. It is God's power that gives us the vision to appreciate and revel in the joys of life, as well as the strength to deal with all its sorrows as well.

1. *Do your find yourself more/less prayerful and meditative in this period of your life as compared to previous periods? Explain.*

_____

_____

_____

_____

_____

2. *In your opinion, who is the holiest person living today? Why do you think so? What qualities does he or she have that you admire? Explain.*

_____

_____

_____

_____

_____

3. *To what degree do you feel that you have a personal relationship with God? Explain.*

_____

_____

_____

_____

_____

_____

4. *What spiritual readings or teachings have impressed you most during the last five years? Describe them, and explain your feelings regarding them.*

_____

_____

_____

_____

_____

_____

5. *Where do you go to feel close to God? What do you do there? Describe.*

_____

_____

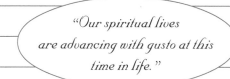

"Our spiritual lives are advancing with gusto at this time in life."

O
ur lifelong spiritual journey toward God is *the* central cohesive energy for all we do and strive toward. Spiritual development gives us the refreshing meaning and the nurturing life purpose that we so fundamentally crave.

Selective Memory

Not all remembrances are healthy and uplifting. Remembrances which simply serve to prove a point, or "grind an axe," are called "selective memory." An example of selective memory would be the older adult who never tires of pointing out that "things were much better years ago." This kind of memory does not help our current maturation, nor does it enhance our spiritual growth. On the contrary, it serves only to stifle and contort the years that could otherwise be filled with new growth and wonder.

Selective memory may also be used as an excuse to cover over personal insufficiency, deceit, past mistakes, grudges, or perceived imperfection. Such selective memory is fragmenting rather than integrating, disengaging rather than participatory, and avoiding rather than positively challenging.

Life Review

In his sensitive book, *Late I Have Loved Thee: Stories of Religious Conversion & Commitment in Later life,* (Paulist Press, New York, 1995), Richard M. Erikson coins the term "biographical reconstruction." This occurs when one's interpretation of the facts of a past event or relationship—not the facts themselves—are modified to reflect the actual reality of the situation more accurately. The individual is able to evolve beyond any distortions that may formerly have rendered him or her partially blind to the truth of the events. Over the years, one's initial appraisal of the situation becomes crystallized into something that takes on a life of its own, apart from the facts. Life review helps us gain a firmer grip on reality by helping us let go of extraneous imagination that may have formerly impaired us.

Discerning the Spiritual Patterns

The central theme of this book is that God has given purpose to our lives. Our response to this gift is to remain open to God's leading hand throughout our life. Most of us can't genuinely discern the hand of God in our lives until we have grown into a more mature state. This last section is designed to be helpful in this one important developmental task of answering the question: "How has God been calling me throughout my life?"

The questions that follow are designed to be pondered, prayed over, and even meditated upon, rather than simply answered. They are big questions—questions which require a well-considered preparation. This is precisely the preparation you have already given yourself by thoughtfully responding to all the questions in this book. Working through this book has given you a background of celestial proportion and positioned you to achieve a new balance, a new centering of your life. Congratulations!

1. *How do you see God's hand at work in each of your six life arenas across the life span?*

   a. School/Career/Work Life

   _____

   _____

   _____

   _____

   _____

   _____

   b. Family Life

   _____

   _____

   _____

   _____

   _____

   _____

   c. Relationship Life

   _____

   _____

   _____

   _____

_____

_____

   d. Self Life

   _____

   _____

   _____

   _____

   _____

   _____

   e. Leisure Life

   _____

   _____

   _____

   _____

   _____

   _____

   f. Spirit Life

   _____

   _____

   _____

   _____

2. What patterns do you discern as you view all six arenas together? Are there overlaps? Do several or more arenas share common themes? Describe.

_____

_____

_____

_____

_____

_____

_____

3. Describe the changes in your prayer life over the decades.

_____

_____

_____

_____

_____

4. What themes and patterns do you see in the way you addressed religious activities over your lifetime? Describe.

_____

_____

5. How has your faith changed over the years?

_____

_____

_____

_____

_____

_____

_____

6. How would you sum up, in a few words, your central "philosophy" of life?

_____

_____

_____

_____

_____

_____

7. To what degree have you achieved a sense of spiritual peace in your life? What has given this to you? Describe.

_____
_____
_____
_____
_____
_____
_____

8. What, if any, spiritual doubts still hang on to your spiritual "coattails" at this time in your life? Describe.

_____
_____
_____
_____
_____

9. As you look back on your life to date, try to identify any spiritual transitions which you experienced; describe them and the personal struggles they may have spawned and/or resolved.

_____
_____
_____
_____
_____
_____
_____

10. From your present vantage point, what do you consider the most significant spiritual experience of your life? Describe what it taught you.

_____
_____
_____
_____
_____

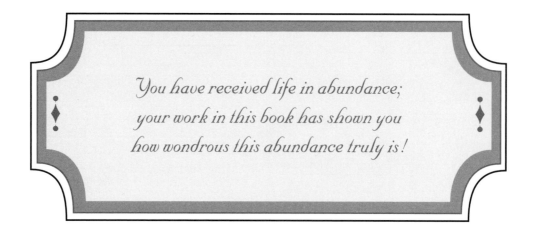

You have received life in abundance;
your work in this book has shown you
how wondrous this abundance truly is!